THE LITTLE BAY MARE

THE TRUE STORY OF A YOUNG GIRL'S STRUGGLE TO RESCUE A NEGLECTED HORSE

BY

LYNDA KAY

To Anna —
Best Wishes!

ISBN: 1-4107-6011-1 (e-book)
ISBN: 1-4107-6010-3 (Paperback)

Library of Congress Control Number: 2003093448

This book is printed on acid free paper.

Printed in the United States of America
Bloomington, IN

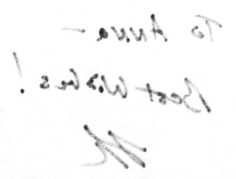

1stBooks – rev. 07/01/03

For my parents, for their unending support,

And

For my husband, for always believing.

YOU CAME TO ME WITH ONLY A
HATRED FOR MANKIND

TIME AND PATIENCE ERASED THE
VENGEANCE FROM YOUR MIND

A WORKING RELATIONSHIP GREW
INTO A LOVING RESPECT

NEVER AGAIN, AT A HUMAN HAND
WOULD YOU KNOW SUCH NEGLECT

EVEN IN PAIN YOU HAVE ALWAYS
SHOWN NOBILITY

IN THIS CONFUSING, STRESSFUL
WORLD YOU HAVE BROUGHT ME
TRANQUILITY

I WONDER WHEN YOU STAND SO
ARDENTLY BY MY SIDE

COULD GOD HAVE PLACED A SOUL
BENEATH THE FLESH OF A HORSE'S
HIDE?

CHAPTER 1

"Please Mom!" I begged incessantly as I showed her the advertisement for horse day camp right in the next town.

It was 1975 and I had just turned 13 years old. I had had a love affair with horses for as long as I could remember. I lived with my parents and three older brothers and an older sister in a small suburban town in upstate New York. We could not keep horses where I lived, but there were several boarding stables nearby. I spent much of my free time grooming lesson horses and cleaning stalls and tack, just to be near the animals I loved. I know that many times the stable owners took advantage of me, but it really didn't matter, I was content just to be around the horses. Occasionally, my parents would drive my friends and I to a 'ride by the hour 'stable and wait for us while we rode. Other parents rarely had the time to take us; somehow my parents made the time. I enjoyed sharing those times with my friends, but I also liked to go by myself. I was such a frequent customer that the stable hands would give me whatever horse I asked for. I always chose a small Quarter horse gelding named "Quentin". He was short in stature, but was wide and muscular. He was responsive and never tried to roll or rub me off on a tree like so many of the other horses did. I

LYNDA KAY

always had a bag full of carrots and apples for him
when I was finished riding. I liked to go during the
week when there were fewer people at the stable. I
would ride out and pretend that I was riding across
the country in the 1800's. I even went in the
winter when there were hardly any customers. The
others missed the best time of year for riding.
When my hour was up, I 'd dismount and watch
the hands lead Quentin away. I'd go into the
lounge area to get a drink and wait for my dad.
When I got home I put my cowboy boots and
chaps in a small closet in the basement. My
mother believed that the closet would keep the
horse odor from spreading to the rest of the house.
She was right, anytime I longed for horses, I could
open the closet door and that wonderful scent
would fulfill me.

I could not remember wanting anything as
much as I wanted to go to summer horse camp.
Instead of being led around on a horse or riding a
hack horse, I could actually learn to ride! The
camp taught hunt seat instead of western, but at
that point I didn't care.

I knew that I would have to present the idea
carefully. My parents always supported us kids in
whatever we did, but horses and riding were met
with some resistance ever since my older sister
broke her pelvis and arm in a riding accident.
Being the youngest of five children had taught me
well to be prepared for any arguments and I guess

my siblings had worn my parents down a bit, too. When my mother said "We'll talk to your father about it", I knew I was on my way to victory.

When my father arrived home from work that afternoon, he was barraged with all the reasons a young girl should go to summer horse camp. I doubt he was prepared for the attack and when he asked what camp cost I had at least fifteen different ways that I was going to raise the money. In the end, my parents paid for most of it anyway.

By the time July arrived that year, I had been waiting anxiously for weeks for horse camp to begin. I could think of nothing else. It was a short drive to the next town to camp and I wasn't sure why I had butterflies in my stomach. As excited as I was about the horses, I was rather shy around new people. We pulled into the long driveway and up to the mess hall that served as the cafeteria. I got out of the car and I watched my dad pull away. I felt a tinge of loneliness, but a camp counselor quickly took charge and herded our small group to a cabin for familiarization with the camp's physical layout and the rules and regulations.

The camp was established and operated in previous years by a lady well known in equestrian circles. The campers were girls and young women largely from good families from all over the East. In spite of the clientele, the facilities, while adequate and sturdy, were not fancy. At this time, control of the camp had been given over to her grandson, Tim.

I suffered impatiently through arts and crafts before we finally made our way through the woods to the barn. As we approached the horses, the smell and sound of them made my heart race with excitement. The horses, all nondescript hack horses, aged and well worn, looked beautiful to me!

I was directed to a large flea-bitten gray, grade horse named "Grey Knight". I was shown how to groom him and clean out his feet. The counselor helped me tack him up and led him into the ring. I put on my hard hat and was given a leg up. He was grand! When I said this to the instructor she laughed as if that was the funniest thing she had ever heard.

"I'm sorry, it's just that no one has ever said that about the gray plug!" She obviously couldn't see him from where I was.

Our stirrups were adjusted and we were shown how to hold the reins. As we walked slowly around the ring we were told many important things about riding and horse care. My instructors were girls not much older than I who worked at camp in exchange for staying and riding there. They were called counselors in training, or C.I.T.s for short. The instruction was simple and many of the instructors were completely disinterested in teaching, but none of that mattered to me. I absorbed all that I could and enjoyed every moment. I loved the feel of the horse underneath me. The way he rocked back and forth with every stride. He was the largest horse I had ever been on and I loved him right away.

The lesson ended all too soon, but I dismounted with a wonderful feeling in my soul. The rest of the day was a huge disappointment as we went from lunch to recreation to swimming. I didn't want to play tennis I wanted to ride. When my dad picked me up that afternoon I was dirty and tired, but excitedly told him about my new favorite horse, Grey Knight. My Dad listened politely and asked a few questions and I'm sure he decided that camp was worth the cost.

It didn't take long for me to figure out how to spend more time at the barn and less at the other activities. No one seemed to care if I made it to arts and crafts and I wasn't interested in making boondoggle key chains. There was always work to do at the barn and the counselors would let me ride more if I helped out with the horses. I got to spend more time with Grey Knight as well.

I met a lot of other girls my age and made friends with a few of them. I met a girl from New York City named Lee. Lee and I spent a lot of time together and were fast becoming good friends. We were an odd match; having been raised worlds apart. Her background and worldly experience fascinated me. I was born and raised in a small suburban town. My father was a teacher at the local high school and my mother was a nurse. We were all healthy, happy and pretty well protected from the outside world. We were not wealthy, but my parents did all they could for us. We were raised with strong morals and strong family connections. Horse camp was a luxury and I knew that.

Lee was raised in New York City, her mother was white and her father was African-American. She and her sister were educated at a boarding school for advanced students. Her parents were divorced and she spent every summer at horse camp. She stayed the entire season and was housed in the cabins. She was an advanced rider and owned her own saddle. She traveled with the show team to local horse shows. Lee rode the better horses and jumped them. I thought she was the luckiest person in the world. It would be years later before I learned that she thought I was the lucky one.

The week of camp ended all too soon. In that time I had become a regular around the barns and the owner agreed to let me work days at camp in order to ride. Some nights I spent on an extra bunk in Lee's cabin and on the weekends Lee would come to my home. I enjoyed her company and felt that my quiet life paled to hers. Lee enjoyed the time spent with my family in my quiet neighborhood. We talked about everything imaginable. It was wonderful to have a trustworthy confidant with whom I could share my fears, hopes and dreams. While my early teens were happy years, I experienced the stresses and anxieties all teens go through. I wanted the freedoms adulthood brought, but was somewhat saddened by the end of a happy, carefree childhood. Lee was sophisticated and independent and seemed so much worldlier than I. At that age I didn't realize that Lee needed the same support and guidance that I did.

One afternoon I walked to junior camp to help with the beginners. It had only been six weeks since I had first arrived, but it felt like years. I had learned so much and had become quite comfortable around the horses. Now I was off to help the new riders tack up, just as I had been helped my first day.

I walked into the barn at junior camp to get a saddle and bridle. Junior barn was where the younger riders took their lessons. The barn at junior camp was used only to house tack and feed. The horses spent the summer in standing stalls outside. The only times I had thought this a bad idea was when it rained. The horses, of course, had no shelter. I picked out the saddle and bridle and carried them toward the horses. The counselors were all standing around a downed horse. The look on their faces told me this was serious. Some of the girls were crying.

"Someone go to the path and stop the kids from coming up here!" the head-riding instructor yelled. With that a counselor headed to the woods to turn back the afternoon students.

"What happened?" I whispered to one of the friendlier counselors.

"Melody's colicking", she replied sadly. I knew that colic is a term used to describe a digestive problem caused by gas or blockage of the intestine. Many times it is fatal in horses.

Melody was an older mare. She was a mousy colored dun with a black stripe down her back and black legs and ears. I loved her color and although she was not a pretty horse, she was always very sweet. She had taught a lot of kids to ride. She was flat out on the ground, moaning and sweating from the pain.

The veterinarian, Dr. James, exited his truck and walked to the mare. I had known Dr. James for years, as he was my own small animal veterinarian. Dr. James was a kind, soft-spoken man, which seemed in conflict given his physical size. He was a big, strong man with large hands and a gentle manner. He listened to the horse's heart, looked at her gums and took her temperature. He gave her an injection to ease the pain. There had to be eight or ten of us girls gathered around watching him. No one spoke. Most of us held our breath.

Over the years of pet ownership, I had several put to sleep. I always had a tough time of it, but seeing this large horse, lying on her side and heaving was more than I could take.

"She's probably beyond saving, but I'll tube her with oil and see", Dr James said to the head riding instructor. He removed a long plastic tube from his bag and a syringe filled with mineral oil. He passed the tube up the mare's nose. He placed the opposite end in his mouth and occasionally blew into it as the tube disappeared up the horse's nose.

"What's he doing?" I quietly inquired.

"He's putting the tube down the horse's throat into her stomach. By blowing into it, he can make sure it's not feeding into her lungs."

"Oh." I said mesmerized by the procedure. Dr. James then put the syringe into the tube and forced the oil into the horse's stomach. We waited twenty long minutes. The mare still lay on her side breathing heavily.

"How long do you want to wait?" Dr. James asked the head instructor. "She's in a lot of pain."

"I guess there is no point in waiting any longer. We can't let her suffer".

With that there was an audible groan from all the girls. Dr. James walked to his truck to get the drugs that would end the mare's life. Before he could return, the mare raised her head. She sat for a moment and then struggled to her feet. She stretched her neck out and bellowed like a cow. She strained and lifted her tail and produced a large quantity of manure. We held our breath; this was a good sign. It meant that she might have passed the blockage. She strained again and this time produced a ball of worms the size of a baseball! I thought I was going to be sick at the sight of it. Dr. James examined the blockage and declared that the mare would be fine.

"When was the last time this horse was wormed?" he demanded. Everyone just looked at each other, camp horse weren't ever wormed, that cost money. Dr. James wormed Melody and within minutes she was back to her old self.

The rest of the summer was rather uneventful after that and before I knew it, it was the end of August. Camp came to an end and Lee went home with a promise to fly up on vacation. At the end of camp every summer, the camp horses were leased to private homes for the winter. There were always some that didn't find homes and stayed in senior barn for the winter. I worked weekends at camp caring for these horses and Tim's own horses. I never cared much for Tim, but I loved working with the horses.

CHAPTER 2

"Do you want to go with me to look at a horse for camp?" It was Tim, the camp owner. I had worked at camp all winter and had been riding a lot. I owed all of that to Tim, and yet I couldn't bring myself to like him or trust him. The sound of his voice always gave me a shiver of fear. I never considered him a horseman. He rode fine horses and competed in shows with his horses. He always did well, but he never seemed to care much for his horses. I had seen him take the whip to his horses for a bad performance and thought him to be quite cruel. I had secretly taken his horses out of their stalls and walked them whenever he put them away hot and lathered. That was another way Tim punished his horses for a poor performance.

I climbed into the truck with Tim and we drove to the farm where the horse for sale was located.

A couple of the leased out camp horses had returned to camp severely neglected. A few of us had nursed them back to health. I was told of horses that became victims of abuse and that never returned to camp, but that didn't prepare me for what I was about to see.

Tim pulled the truck into the short driveway and stopped at the house. The house was well maintained with a freshly mown lawn and immaculate flowerbeds along the house. There was a pretty white board fence that stretched across the lawn to the right of the driveway. I stepped out of the truck and walked to the fence. There was a gray, fourteen-hand pony in the small pasture. She was so grossly overweight that she had trouble walking. I extended my hand to her as she approached the fence. Out of the corner of my eye I noticed movement in the shadows of the trees in a back corner of the pasture. Into the sunlight stepped a bay horse about fourteen hands tall as well. She was so thin and pathetic looking; I gasped at the sight of her. The hollows over her eyes sunk in to reveal the skeletal structure of her face. The eyes themselves were sad, with a distant, hopeless expression. She was sway-backed and her chest was so small and shrunken, it forced her knees together. Her feet were curling upward and she walked very carefully. Her prominent withers supported a shrunken ewe-neck that did not look as though it could support her head. Her coat was long and wavy even though it was April and the horses that had remained in camp were shedding out. Even the long coat could not conceal the protruding ribs and hipbones. She had no rump to speak of, just bones covered by a thin layer of skin.

I could feel the tears welling up in my eyes and the anger burning in my stomach. As Tim and the owner approached, I turned to look into the face of the human being that was responsible for such misery. This small older man pointed to the little bay, "that's the one, that bay over there." I looked at him and slowly realized that this man had no idea that this horse was close to death.

"How much have you been feeding them?" Tim asked.

"I give them eight quarts of grain a day, plus hay," the owner answered.

"Don't you see that the gray is getting all the food?" Tim asked.

"Yeah, huh, she's the bossy one," the owner said. As Tim and the owner continued their conversation, I climbed through the fence. The little bay mare pricked her ears and timidly approached me, all the while keeping an eye on the gray for any threat of attack. I stroked her neck as she gently sniffed me over with her muzzle. Her coat fell out in clumps as I petted her. The skin beneath was dry and scaly and dandruff particles came out with the hair. Her bone structure was solid and her conformation was good. This horse couldn't have been like this forever; she must have been well cared for in her earlier years. She had a lot of graying around her muzzle and eyes and I realized that this horse was advanced in years. How sad this creature was spending her remaining years in this condition. I saw that she had a dropped hip as well. At the time I didn't know exactly what it was, but I knew it was a condition that may have led her down this road. I wondered if whoever had owned her previously would be horrified at her condition now.

"C'mon Lyn," Tim called. I gave her one last pat and saw all the filthy crud on my hands from her. None of that mattered now, though, she'd be coming to camp and I'd make sure she got the best of everything.

"When are we coming back for her?" I asked Tim, once we were in the truck.

"We're not," Tim answered flatly. "I can't spend good money on an old horse in such bad condition. She'll probably die, anyway." I looked at him in total disbelief. Hadn't he seen what I had?

"You can't just leave her there!" I pleaded. "Did you see how sweet she is? She'd make a great camp horse."

"The man wants twenty five dollars for her, I told him he couldn't pay me to take her."

"Well, we have to call the S. P. C. A. at least," I told him.

"It's none of our business, don't get them involved," Tim told me in no uncertain terms.

"Look, I know you don't understand, but I have a business to run. I can't take everyone else's problem. Life is cruel." Tim told me.

Easter vacation came a week later and although I was busy at camp riding the left over camp horses, I couldn't stop thinking about the little bay mare. I would lie awake on cold nights, unable to sleep with the thought of her going hungry. I couldn't understand how someone in Tim's position, with plenty of stalls and hay and feed, could leave that poor horse to die. I was beginning to feel a genuine hatred for Tim. Not everything should be about money. I never knew that someone could build a career and lifestyle around horses and remain so indifferent to them.

The next day my parents drove me to the airport to pick up Lee. She was going to spend Easter vacation with us. Lee and I would spend most of our time at camp and the rest of the time filling each other in on all the issues that were important to teen-age girls.

As we drove home from the airport I told Lee all about the little bay mare. My parents explained again why we couldn't afford to keep a horse. It seemed that no one else cared about that poor horse but me. I had begged my parents to let me get her, but I knew there was no way that they could afford to. I also knew they would have let me if they could have.

The next day Lee and I went out to camp to work and ride. Lee was a good rider and she usually rode one of Tim's better horses. I admit I was always a little jealous of her ability, although she never gave me any reason to be. Lee was a very kind and caring person and she never made me feel inadequate in any way.

That year no one had taken Grey Knight home for the winter, so he had become a bit of a project for me. The big, stout, gray had always been used as a beginner's mount and was affectionately nicknamed "The Grey Plug". He was quite a character and had a lot of personality. During the days at camp he would feign lameness until it was determined that he was too sore to ride and he was turned out for the day. As the pasture gate closed, he would gallop and buck with delight and although no lameness could be detected, there was no catching him. The next day the charade would start all over again.

I had spent the last several months riding Grey Knight and was even jumping him over small cross-rails. I was the only person riding him and he responded to the one on one attention. He was responsive to my leg aids and had become a pleasure to ride. He was well fed and groomed and the regular work had developed his long under-used muscles. Lee hardly recognized him when she saw him. I was not much of a rider, having had little instruction, but I learned a lot from Grey Knight. Most of the time I rode him bareback for lack of a saddle. I had even been jumping him bareback. I was what they called a "seat of the pants" rider. I could climb on and ride nearly any horse; I just didn't look too good doing it. I really had no business jumping with my lack of experience, but that didn't stop me. The big gray would canter to the fence, I'd get a little ahead of him and he'd stop and dump me over the fence. I couldn't count the number of times he did this. I was too inexperienced to know how to correct it, so I just kept trying. I think Grey Knight finally got tired of dumping me and decided to jump the fence. We did a lot of jumping after that and I really enjoyed it. I was quite proud of what I had done with Grey Knight and even Tim commented on how well the horse was going. "We'll have to move him up to the more advanced group this year", he told me. It was at that moment I realized that Grey Knight would not be mine forever. When camp resumed that summer Grey Knight would be ridden by lots of other girls several times a day. I felt sorry for him, camp was hard on the horses and he was probably better off being used for beginners. At least they wouldn't work him so hard.

The following day as Lee and I walked into the barn, we saw a small, thin pony tied in a standing stall at the far end of the barn. We walked past the four box stalls where Tim's horses were and down along the rows of standing stalls where Grey Knight and the camp horses were.

"What horse is it?" Lee asked. I squinted while my eyes adjusted to the darkness in the barn. The horse had a small metal clip in her mane, proving she had been tested for Equine Infectious Anemia, a highly contagious disease. The clip told us she was a new horse. As we approached her, the little horse nickered softly to us.

"Wow, she looks *terrible*!" Lee said.

"Oh, hey! It's that horse we looked at! It must be her!" I was glad to see her, but the sight of her still shocked me.

"My God, who could do this to an animal?" Lee asked. I told her all about the nice house and yard and the fat pony stabled with her.

"You mean to tell me that they couldn't tell that this horse wasn't getting any food? What are they blind?"

"No, just ignorant", Tim answered as he walked up behind us. "They didn't know any better. I don't think they meant to be cruel, they just thought something was wrong with the horse."

"Why wouldn't this horse fight for her share of the food? I mean she was starving to death." I asked.

"Horses have a pecking order, some are more aggressive, they are the herd leaders. Those horses eat first and drive the others away. This mare, here, is timid and she waited her turn. Unfortunately, by the time it was her turn, there was nothing left to eat," Tim explained to me. "What they should have done, is separate the horses at feeding time."

"Why did you change your mind and go get her?" I asked him.

"The owner called and told me that I could have the horse if I came and got her. I thought she'd make a good project for you. If she survives, you can get her in shape for camp. Dr. James will be out in a couple of hours to look at her."

While we waited for Dr. James, I began caring for my new horse. I found a couple of buckets that were in pretty good shape and scrubbed them clean. I hung one on either side of her stall with bailing twine. I filled one with clean, fresh water and got my brushes from the tack room. I began to carefully rub the mare with my currycomb. Although it was made of soft rubber, she pulled away from any pressure. Her hair came out in clumps and fell to the ground. The white dandruff came to the surface as I brushed. She leaned against my brush any time that I came to an especially itchy spot. As I rubbed along her mane, she leaned into me and stretched her neck out in pleasure. The mane was thin and brittle and even though I brushed gently, some of it came out in my brush. The mane was matted and greasy at the base. The entire time I worked on her, I couldn't help but wonder why Tim had done this for me. I couldn't think of a single time that he had ever done anything that didn't benefit him in some way.

"How's it going?" Lee asked as she walked over to us.

"Look at this ", I answered, showing her the hair in clumps on the ground. "This poor horse.

19

She's really sweet though". I could tell by the look on Lee's face that she thought this horse was in serious trouble.

"She'll be OK, now, right?" I asked, hopefully.

"I don't know, she's in rough shape. Let's hope for the best and see what the vet says".

When Lee left, I leaned over to the mare, "I won't let anything bad ever happen to you again. I promise", I told her. I gave her a kiss on her star and went to wait for Dr. James.

Lee and I sat on the porch outside of the tack room to eat our lunch and wait for the vet. My brother, John, had been hired as a part-time maintenance worker at camp and he and Dave, another worker, sat with us. It was cold and rainy. April in upstate New York could be fickle. The weather was always very changeable. I watched the rain drip off of the roof while the others talked. I was hoping that Dr. James would come before it was time to leave. I wanted to talk to him myself.

The guys got up to go back to work. "I'll be back around four to get you", John called, as he and Dave got into the truck.

"That's quite a truck!" Lee said.

"Yeah, John loves it", I told her. The truck was a 1968 Chevy that had seen better days, but was my seventeen-year-old brother's pride and joy. I had spent my entire life tagging along after my older brother and he had always been tolerant.

This truck gave him the freedom to go where he pleased and he drove me around a lot as well.

As we walked into the barn, I heard a car pull up outside. I looked out the window hoping that it was Dr. James, but it was only Tim. I went back to cleaning the camp tack. Tim came in the tack room and asked us how we were doing. We spent a lot of time getting the saddles and bridles cleaned and sorted for camp use. Another car pulled in. This time, Dr. James stepped out of his truck.

We turned the lights on for him and showed him to the new horse. Dr. James approached the horse's head and gently stroked her face. He silently opened her mouth and shown his light in to examine her teeth. He closed her mouth and looked into her eyes. Next he ran his hands along her throat and over her back. The spine rose above her ribcage, protruding grossly under her skin. He ran his hands along her sway back and down her legs. He stepped back and looked at her. He pursed his lips before he spoke.

"This is going to be a camp horse?" he asked Tim.

"Yeah, she's Lyn's project for now, but if she makes it, she'll have to go to work. I can't keep anything that doesn't earn its' keep", Tim responded.

Dr. James turned his gaze to me. I had known him for many years. He had comforted me many times over the loss of a pet. I knew that look; he was choosing his words carefully.

"This mare's been starved a long time," he said. "I'm surprised that she has survived this long. On top of that, she's at a very advanced age. Once they get to be twenty or so, it's difficult to tell just how old, but I'd guess she's in her late twenties. She's so old; some of her molars are gone. A horse's teeth continue to grow their whole life. They wear them down chewing their food. This means that even if she had been fed properly, she would have had trouble chewing."

He looked directly at me while I tried to understand what he said, "when horses have been starved this severely for this length of time, their internal organs are affected. They can no longer function properly or completely."

OK, OK, I thought to myself, but what do we do to help her now?

Tim broke the silence, "what do you suggest?"

"I'm sorry, but I really think that the most humane thing to do is euthanize her", Dr. James replied, almost apologetically. Tears streamed down my face and dripped onto my hands as I clenched her halter. The world seemed to spin around me. I frantically searched my mind for an argument. I couldn't let this happen, not now, after all of this. I felt a hand on my shoulder. It was Lee, trying to comfort me. Dr. James began to collect his equipment and put it in his bag. In desperation

I blurted out "couldn't we give her some time and see how she does? You said yourself that you couldn't believe she's still alive! Couldn't we just try for a little while?" I turned to Tim, "I'll pay for her food, it won't cost you a thing. I'll take care of her. Please, couldn't we try? Doesn't she deserve a chance?" I pleaded with Tim and prayed that just this once he might have a little compassion, if not for her, then for me.

"I guess we could see, but if she doesn't make a camp horse she's gone." I thanked God for answering my prayer and turned to Tim, "You won't be sorry," I promised him.

Dr. James explained how best to care for her and stressed that she must be brought back to health slowly.

"When horses are in a severe state of malnutrition they may give up and lay down to die. If she goes down, she's done. Don't get your hopes up too high, she may still die." Dr. James vaccinated her and floated her teeth with a large rasp that evens out the points, making it easier to chew. He then passed a tube up her nose and into her stomach the same way as he had done with Melody when she colicked. This time, however, he inserted deworming medicine into it, to rid the mare of parasites.

I selected the best hay I could find and placed it in front of her. The mare picked through it carefully, selecting the tastiest pieces of hay. Her feeding program would involve returning grain to her diet very slowly, so as not to overwhelm her deprived system. We began with small amounts of sweet feed mixed with beet pulp that had been soaked in warm water to soften it. Beet pulp is a high fiber feed made from the stalks of sugar beets. It was a popular item at the time to add to the diet of low weight horses. I fed the mare small amounts of the mixture frequently throughout the day and she gobbled it up and looked for more.

Within a couple of weeks, the mare began to blossom. Her weight hadn't changed much at this point, but her eyes had a new shine to them. Her ragged coat was shedding and her summer coat was coming in shiny and lighter in color. Her hooves had been trimmed and she was visibly perking up. I began to see her real personality and not just the dull responses of a dying horse. She nickered to me whenever she saw me and we began to bond in a wonderful way. I loved her with all of my heart.

CHAPTER 3

In all of this time, the horse had not had a name. When Tim had first picked her up, he had never asked her name and actually, a new start should bring a new name anyway. During this time I was reading a novel about Native Americans. The main character was an Apache Indian and his horse's name was "Nejaunee", which was a word that was supposed to mean friend in Apache. I don't know if the word really meant that, or was simply made up by the author, but it seemed a lovely, appropriate name for my new friend. I wasn't prepared for all the quizzical looks and snickers that the name brought, but that didn't change my mind. I was resigned to repeating it several times whenever someone asked her name. I guess it would have made more sense if the horse was a breed with Native American beginnings, like an Appaloosa, But I liked it and in the end that's all that mattered.

By the end of May the mare had gained a lot of her strength back and was even energetic on cool mornings. Her coat glistened in good health. Her weight, although slow to return, was increasing. She was still quite thin and would probably never regain all the weight she should, but at least there was some meat covering her bones now. She was turned out in the pasture regularly for exercise and was acting more and more like the free spirit that I thought she was. She would trot out to her pasture buddies with her head and tail high in the air.

I still watched closely to ensure that the other horses didn't pick on her, but she seemed happy and content in her new life. I was thrilled and thankful that everything was going so well. I spent most of my free time at camp. I hitched a ride with my brother when he worked and had my parents take me when he didn't. There were very few riders at camp and it was as if she were mine and mine alone. No one else had any interest in an old skinny horse that you couldn't ride yet. The other girls had their own horses or took lessons from Tim on his jumpers and they considered Nejaunee and I peasants. That was fine with me. I had her and that was all that mattered.

My parents took me to a local tack shop and helped me purchase a few necessary items for the horse. I loved just going into the store and looking at all the beautiful saddles and equipment. I bought a new halter to replace the old rope halter Nejaunee had come with. The halter was green nylon with white stitching. I bought a selection of brushes and combs for her grooming and a western saddle pad. I had found an old western saddle in the attic at camp and always wanted to ride western. I wasn't very experienced at riding hunt seat and western seemed easier, at least to get started. I knew Nejaunee would never be capable of jumping anyway. My Dad always bought a copy of The Quarter Horse Journal, just because he couldn't believe you could buy a magazine with several hundred pages for a dollar. The horses in that magazine certainly looked nothing like mine. They were the most beautiful horses I had ever seen.

When I returned to camp the following week, Tim told me it was time to get my horse ready for camp.

"Remember our deal," he said, "I got this horse to be a camp horse, she has to be able to be ridden."

I had gotten so drawn into my little world that centered on the little mare, I had forgotten there would come a time when others would ride Nejaunee. She would no longer be just mine. I knew that if she didn't work out, Tim would send her off without a thought of either of us. I had seen it before. Junior camp had been closed and all the beginners now rode at senior barn. Junior barn had become an overgrown pasture and was used as a turnout for horse's who had outlived their usefulness. From there, the killers from the slaughterhouses picked them up and hauled them away. I never understood how come so few people at camp seemed to care about the destiny of these animals. I knew Tim saw it as a part of the business, but even the other campers and counselors seemed to accept this practice. Horses that didn't work out, horses with chronic lameness and those too old to ride made the trip to junior camp. Some of these horses had been trusted and faithful camp horses for years, giving all they had every summer. They went to the same homes every winter, yet no one seemed to care. I guess that most people didn't know what had become of their favorite horse. It always seemed to me that those horses had earned their retirements and that they deserved better.

I knew that if Nejaunee did not work out, that was where she was headed. I decided it was far better to share her than to lose her to the killers. I would do all I could to train her properly.

I had received very little riding instruction at camp, let alone any instruction on training horses. I had watched Tim and some of the advanced riders do some training with the younger or 'green' horses, but I didn't even fully understand the process. I read everything I could in hopes of gaining some insight, but that in no way prepared me for the actual process. Looking back now, the only reason Nejaunee and I survived her training is that first of all, she had been broke to ride, and secondly, she had a very tolerant temperament.

Lee came to camp early that year and was there well before camp opened. She helped me a great deal with the training, but we all learned as we went. Lee and I decided to start the training by lunging Nejaunee to strengthen her long underused muscles. It was also a good way to teach her verbal cues from the ground. Lunging is a process that involves having the trainer stand in the middle of a circle with a long line attached to the horse's halter or bridle. The horse proceeds around the circle created by the line at various gaits. The trainer encourages the horse to move forward with the help of a long whip.

Lee went to the middle of the riding ring and held the line and the whip. I positioned myself on the opposite side of Nejaunee and attached a lead line to that side of her halter. Lee commanded the horse to move forward with a verbal cluck and a tap of the whip. I walked forward with the horse to teach her what Lee was requesting. We repeated this exercise at the walk and trot several times. Nejaunee did not understand what we wanted, but did her best to oblige us. After about twenty minutes, I had had enough and we decided to quit before Nejaunee became fatigued. I wanted her to have a good attitude towards training so we didn't push her too hard the first few times. I believed it was important to quit on a good note.

In the meantime, Lee had begun to ride Grey Knight in order to prepare him for the advanced riders. Tim was going to move him up. I was proud of what I had done with Grey Knight and thought he looked great. I was glad Lee was riding him. She always cared about the horses she rode and was kind to them. I was a little jealous,

29

because I knew I wouldn't be riding him anymore, but I had Nejaunee to worry about. Grey Knight had been a camp horse a long time and I knew he would be okay.

Opening day of camp was rapidly approaching. Tim had hired me as a counselor in training for the summer, so I could continue to work in the barn and stay at camp. It wouldn't be long before the other counselors arrived and began to prepare for camp. Tim threatened to send Nejaunee to the killers, so Lee and I pressed on.

We continued to teach Nejaunee to lunge. I knew we were missing something because the horse didn't seem to be getting it. Whenever I didn't lead her, Nejaunee would turn to face us. I didn't know how to correct it, so we pressed on and Nejaunee seemed to slowly comprehend.

One day Tim pulled up as we were working the mare. I knew he'd have something mean to say, he usually did. My cheeks flushed with apprehension. Tim leaned on the fence and watched Lee and I struggle in our lunging attempts. Then he stepped through the fence, walked to Lee and took the line and whip from her.

"Unhook your lead line", he commanded. I did what I was told, however regretfully and stepped away. I knew this was not going to be pleasant. Lee came over and stood next to me. One look at her face told me she thought the same. The little mare stood where she was and looked attentively at Tim. She was completely trusting and had a sweet expression on her face. Tim clucked to her. She took one step and turned in to face Tim. Without warning, Tim laid the whip across Nejaunee's hips full force. The horse jumped forward, then stood and looked at Tim, her eyes wide with fear. Tim clucked and whipped her again. And again. And again. Nejaunee tucked her tail between her legs, dropped her head and stood her ground. The lashings kept coming. I gripped the rail of the fence and willed her to move forward. I could see the welts rising on her rump. Every strike of the whip made her back dip, but she would not take a step. The more Tim lost his temper, the harder he whipped her. She stood and bared it. I knew that she didn't know she should move forward. Her expression told me this was not the first time she had been whipped.

I pleaded from the fence, too afraid of Tim to enter the ring, "Please Tim! *Please* stop!"

"This horse needs to learn who's in charge!" he yelled back. Then he positioned himself a little more behind her and whipped her across the hocks. Nejaunee leapt into the air several times in order to escape the whip. She pulled back against the line with all her might in a desperate attempt to free herself. Finally she lunged forward and ran for her life. Tim braced himself against her pull while she ran wildly at the end of the line, frantically looking for an escape route. Tim had dropped the whip and was holding the line with both hands. The anger seethed inside of me. I stood helpless at the fence, too afraid to move. I knew what he was doing was wrong. I didn't have to be a horse trainer to see that. Nejaunee stopped and pulled desperately at the end of the line. She planted her front feet, braced herself and shook her head from side to side trying to escape. I wished the halter would break. At that moment I broke free from my fears of Tim that had paralyzed me and ran to the horse. I grabbed her halter and unsnapped the lunge line. She straightened but still glared at Tim, her eyes fearful. She was sweating and breathing so hard I was afraid she might collapse. Her body was tense and her flared nostrils were scarlet in color from the exertion.

"There! That's how you train a horse!" Tim said as he threw down the line and walked away. I glared at him until he was in his truck and driving away. Lee walked over and picked up the lead line and brought it to me. She gently ran her hands over the welts on the horses rump and legs. "You better walk her, she's going to be stiff tomorrow." Lee and I looked at each other but neither of us spoke. Words were not necessary. We had witnessed an incredible act of cruelty. If that was how you trained a horse, I wanted no part of it. There had to be a better way.

I walked Nejaunee until she was cool. I hosed her off with cool water. I let the water run gently over her welts to ease the pain. I put antibiotic salve on the open welts and rubbed her legs with liniment. Through tearful eyes I told Nejaunee how sorry I was. I blamed myself over and over again for not stopping the abuse. I filled her water bucket and gave her some hay. Lee and I fed the other horses and finished our chores in silence. Lee returned home with me to spend the night.

That night when Lee and I were in my bedroom, she told me, "Don't blame yourself, there was nothing you could have done".

"I feel so bad. That horse didn't deserve that. I know we weren't getting very far with her, but what he did *can't* be right."

"She was doing okay with what we were doing. I hope she's not really frightened now. That will make the training harder", Lee said. "We'll have to be really careful not to let Tim see us working her. We can't let that happen again, Lyn."

So in the following weeks Lee stood guard at the driveway in order to alert me to any vehicle coming up the drive. We had a few false alarms, but for the most part it worked well. We went back to our own slow methods and Nejaunee held no grudges. She was lunging beautifully before long and I was soon riding her. I rode in the western saddle and a bridle I had found as well. I was quite a sight with my long unruly hair stuffed under an English hard hat and my skinny horse. I rode her on the trails through camp and even jumped her

33

over some of the small logs on the paths. She didn't know much, but neither did I. She neck reined a little and moved forward when I gave her a squeeze with my legs and that was good enough for me.

CHAPTER 4

The following week the counselors hired for summer camp began to arrive. The quiet and private barn that I had enjoyed for the past several months became a busy, hectic place. The counselors moved in and changed things on a daily basis. There was a lot to get done in preparation for opening day of camp, when close to a hundred campers would arrive. The horses returned from their winter homes and we had to match each horse to a saddle, bridle and girth. The farrier came daily to trim and shoe the horses. Each horse was also assigned a stall. I was careful to put Nejaunee in the end stall, with a wall on one side and a quiet horse on the other. She was still easily bullied and in the standing stalls the horses had easy access to each other.

My brother, John was busy as well, working as a maintenance employee. He provided me with a ride to and from camp each day.

Lee was assigned to her cabin and riding times. I was assigned to a different cabin and was responsible for the supervision of four 9 and 10 year old girls. My time was consumed by the stable work and I only saw the campers at night. I was only 14 years old myself and wasn't prepared to over -see four little girls.

By this time, Nejaunee was riding well and although she was still quite thin, she no longer looked starved. She was placed in the beginner classes and assigned English tack. Whenever I rode her I still used the western saddle and bridle and found her to be an energetic, almost high-strung animal. I rode her whenever an instructor took the riders on a trail ride. The instructor needed someone to follow behind the students in order to help in case there was trouble with any of the mounts. I always took full advantage of this situation and before long, I was the one they always asked to ride with them. I loved riding the trails. We would go through the creek and along the wooded trails to the hunt course. The hunt course was an open field with several natural jumps constructed of logs and timbers. Once there, the instructor would give the lesson and then we would return to the barn. Some days I rode out several times with different classes. It didn't seem much like work to me, but many of the other counselors-in-training didn't want to go. I was allowed a one-hour lesson a day. I now rode in a novice class and seldom used Nejaunee for my lesson. I sometimes rode Grey Knight if he had not been used that day, but most times I rode one of the others. I always rode English for my classes and was progressing with my jumping. The days were long and the work hard. The summer sun could be very hot, especially when you had to wear jeans all day, but I loved every minute. The afternoon chores were the hardest and hottest. Many of the camp horses were turned out in the pasture for the night. This accomplished several things. The horses got some necessary turn out, the stalls stayed cleaner and it was cooler outside. We would fill the water troughs and load bales of hay into wheelbarrows to take to the pasture to supplement what little grass there was. I would load four bales onto my wheelbarrow, when most took only two or three. Then I had to push the wheelbarrow uphill to get to the pasture. After weeks of doing all of this work I became strong and fit. I ate a lot and slept well every night.

Many of the campers came and went, but one thing always remained constant. Tim gave preferential treatment to the campers with money and those without fended for themselves. I did my best to avoid Tim. Camp was a busy place and I rarely saw him.

Nejaunee was not doing too well as a lesson horse and the instructors were using her less and less. Luckily, Tim was too busy to notice.

One Friday afternoon I was in the barn grooming Nejaunee. The others had all gone to dinner and I was alone while I waited for John to pick me up.

"So, this must be, uh, how do you say her name?" A very attractive, soft-spoken woman asked me as she approached us.

Caught off-guard, a small amount of panic crept into my stomach. It must have shown on my face because her next words were soft and friendly.

"I'm Amanda, Tim's cousin. I've heard about your rescue and rehabilitation efforts. She looks like she's had tough time. She's lucky she found you." *She* found *me*. What an interesting way of putting it. I had thought that I had found her.

My defenses lowered, I replied," Uh…hi, sorry, you startled me. I'm Lyn; this is Nejaunee, Nay-shawn-ee. I call her Nauj for short."

"Well, I didn't mean to disturb you. I'll be here for the rest of the summer, so I guess I'll see you later". Then she added, "don't let them get you down. You're doing a great thing, helping that mare".

I watched her walk out of the barn. I collected my things, gave Nauj a kiss and waited outside for John.

CHAPTER 5

I continued to work hard all summer. Amanda proved to be a wealth of information and I drove her crazy asking her horse-related questions. She was a refined woman with a kind heart and she was a top equestrian. She was sympathetic to my situation with Nejaunee and always offered all the help she could. I liked her very much.

Late one afternoon while I was waiting at the barn for my ride, Tim approached me.

"What are we going to do about your horse?" he asked me.

"What do you mean?" I asked, feeling fear rise in my chest.

"They tell me we're not able to use her for lessons."

"She still needs some time. She's doing well and she looks great."

"Remember what I told you. Any horse that doesn't work doesn't stay. You can't be the only one who rides her. Tomorrow I want you to take her up to junior pasture and turn her out with that Thoroughbred colt. You can ride her until they go to auction", Tim told me. It was that easy for him. He cared that little for not only the horse, but for me as well.

I had worked long and hard all summer with very little reward. I cleaned stalls, hauled hay, fixed fence and did whatever else needed to be done. I worked for free all winter long and this was my payback. The world was so unfair. Who was he to decide the fate of the horse that I loved?

When he left I pressed my face into Nejaunee's soft black mane and wept. I had promised her that I would never let this happen, now what could I do? I stroked her muzzle and offered words of comfort. I know she didn't understand what was going on, but that brought me little comfort. She deserved a safe, warm place to live, not to be hauled off to a slaughterhouse.

I left the barn in search of Lee. I told her what Tim had said. As I cried, she tried to console me with ideas to save the horse.

"We could call the S.P.C.A. or find her a home", she offered.

"Who would want her? And Tim won't let the S.P.C.A. have her." The hopelessness of the situation sank in. I couldn't bare the thought of her being hauled away.

The next morning, I did what I was told. I saddled and bridled Nejaunee and rode her to junior barn. Since camp no longer used junior barn, the riding rings had become overgrown and were now used as turnout for horses on their way to slaughter. I un-tacked her and led her into the pasture. The Thoroughbred colt sniffed her and they both squealed, but that seemed to be the end of it. At least he hadn't kicked at her. The colt was a horse Tim had gotten from the racetrack. He had a stifle injury that would not heal. I filled the water trough and went into the barn to look for some grain. I searched the barn but didn't find any feed at all. I petted Nejaunee once more and left in search of the head-riding instructor.

"Karen," I yelled when I saw her, "There's no grain at junior barn for the horses there".

"Those horses are on their way to slaughter, there's no sense in feeding them. They'll survive on the grass that's there."

"They'll be hungry! Can't I take them some? I'll take care of them, no one else has to be bothered", I asked her.

"Absolutely not!" she told me. "If Tim ever found out, he'd kill us both. I know how you feel about that horse, but that's the way things go, you can't save them all."

Oh, if I had a dime for every time I had gotten that little piece of wisdom! So let's see, that means that we should never try to save *any*? So many of these people seemed to believe that animals were ours to use and then throw away as we saw fit. I often wondered if that was what God was thinking when he gave us dominion over them. I guess that I was under the somehow mistaken belief that He meant we had a responsibility *to* them as well. (Now there's a curious thought!)

I knew arguing was futile and left.

I found my brother digging a trench for water run-off behind senior barn. I told him what happened with Nejaunee.

"Oh, I'm so sorry, Lyn. I know how much she means to you," he said.

"Listen, John, before you go home tonight do you think we could take a bag of grain up to junior barn? The horses up there don't have anything to eat."

"I'm really busy right now, why don't you ask Dave?" John suggested.

"Tim says we're not supposed to feed them, but I can't let them go hungry. Please!"

"If we get caught I'll get fired," John said flatly.

"If you won't help, I'll haul it up there in a wheelbarrow if I have to!"

"Okay. I got about another hour. Find out where Tim is and we'll do it then. I better not lose my job."

An hour later we loaded a hundred pound bag of grain into his truck. Tim was at his house and the rest of the camp was at supper. John drove to junior camp and unloaded the grain for me. I fed the horses and waited for Nejaunee to finish. I filled the trough with water and got in the truck to go home.

"When are they coming for those horses?"

"I don't know. I'm afraid every day when I walk up here that they'll be gone." I starred out the window and rode home in silence.

CHAPTER 6

I spent the next few days riding my bike all over town searching for stables that might allow me to work in exchange for Nejaunee's board. I hoped that if I could find a place to board her, my parents might give in and let me keep her. The stables that I had approached were small, private stables and although most were sympathetic to my predicament, they didn't have enough work for me.

I pulled into the driveway of a stable a mile from my house and set down my bike. There were several horses turned out in a large pasture. The barn was a beautiful old gable roof barn that had originally housed Angus beef cattle. There was a large concrete courtyard and a run-in shed for the animals in bad weather. There was a small riding ring set within the pasture. Across from the barn there was a run down shed with a tin roof that also housed horses. The facility had not been cared for and much of it was in disrepair, but even that could not detract from the grandeur of the farm.

I approached the house and prepared myself for another disappointment while I knocked on the door. An older woman answered the door and listened quietly while I repeated my well-rehearsed offer. The woman introduced herself as Mrs. Moore and asked me in.

"What kind of work can you do?" She asked.

"Anything, Anything at all. I can clean stalls, groom, stack hay, anything." I answered.

"Well, I lease the barn to a trainer, Carol. She runs the barn, but maybe you could work around the house in exchange for horse board. Can you mow the lawn and trim the hedges and things like that?"

"Oh, yes! I can do all of those things. I help mow the lawn at home. I'm pretty strong for a girl," I answered excitedly.

"Well we charge fifty dollars a month for the stall. That doesn't include feed, hay or bedding and you have to clean and feed your horse yourself," Mrs. Moore told me.

"I can do it? I can have the job!?" I asked excitedly.

"I think it could work out. I'll figure out a work schedule for you that will cover the cost of the board," she told me.

I rode my bike home, my adrenaline rushing the entire way. I ran up to my room to plan my discussion with my parents. I knew that I had to be prepared. I had to present a flawless plan on how I could afford to care for the horse. I sat down and figured out the cost of hay and grain and bedding for the stall. I averaged my monthly income including allowance and babysitting jobs. I didn't care if it took every dime I had; the horse was worth it. Elton John Albums and Breyer horse models would have to wait.

That night after dinner, I asked my Mom and Dad if I could talk to them. We sat at the kitchen table and I explained my plan. My parents asked a few questions and a few "what ifs", but I was prepared, and answered them all. I remained hopeful when they didn't dismiss the idea completely.

"This stable down the road will let you work for the board then?" my Dad asked again.

"Yeah, she says she has a lot of yard work that I could do."

"How much does Tim want for the horse?" he asked.

"I haven't asked him yet, but he got her for free," I added.

"Well, find out how much the horse is and how much you have saved. We aren't promising anything, but your mother and I will discuss it. We would love to let you have this horse, but we have to think about all the possibilities." my Dad said.

"We try to give you kids all that we can, but this is a big responsibility. We need to consider all that's involved, honey," my Mom added.

"I'll do anything I have to do to get her out of there, Mom."

"We'll think about it, dear."

I went to my room feeling hopeful. I prayed for help and then lay down. I was exhausted. I felt as if I was on an emotional roller coaster. I knew if my parents said 'no', it was over for Nejaunee.

The following week was slow at camp and Tim threatened to send Nejaunee to the killers on a regular basis. If what I felt for him wasn't hatred, it was close.

I finally got up the courage to ask Tim about buying the horse.

"Well, she's worth around six hundred dollars for meat," Tim told me.

"I can't afford that, Tim. Couldn't you give me a break? You got her for free," I pleaded.

"Well, I have an investment in her now. I fed her and paid for a vet and a farrier, too. Six hundred dollars, that's her price," he said.

If looks could kill, I thought as I walked away. Where would I ever get six hundred dollars? My savings totaled one hundred and twenty seven dollars. I walked up to junior barn and crawled through the fence. I sat in the grass near the horses and watched them contentedly eating grass. What a blessing that they remained unaware of their fate. I placed my head in my hands and sobbed. How much have I cried over this horse? This entire situation was so unfair. Why me? Why her? Why had God brought her to me only to see this happen? I always believed that things happened for a reason, but I couldn't find a reason behind all this pain. I sat there for quite a while. The horses would occasionally give me a curious look and then go back to eating. It should have been a pleasant moment with the late summer breeze, the smell of grass and the sound of horses chewing and blowing. These things had always brought pleasure to me before. Sitting with them now only brought a feeling of immense sadness.

Both horses snapped their heads up and focused on something behind me. I turned in that direction wiping the tears from my face and hoping it wasn't Tim. I didn't want him to see me cry.

"I thought I might find you here," it was Amanda. I slumped back down in the grass.

"When is she going?" she asked as she sat down beside me.

"I don't know, Tim likes to torture me with it. The sooner the better I guess."

"I thought you had a line on a boarding stable," she said.

"I did, but Tim won't sell her for less than six hundred dollars. I don't have that much money. If I did I swear I'd buy her." I said.

"He won't give you that horse?" she asked angrily.

"No, she's not worth anything to him either. He just likes to play games," I told her. "Every day I come here fearing the worst. I say good-bye every night when I leave," with that I broke into tears again. Amanda patted my shoulder gently.

"When she's gone, so am I," I said. "I won't be back. I can't take it anymore. I don't want to be here. I'll miss everyone and the horses, but it'll be different for me. I hate Tim; I'll always hate him. I sure as hell won't work for him, he can get some other sap."

"I wouldn't blame you for leaving, but it would be a shame if you let him drive you away from horses entirely, you love them so," Amanda said.

"Well, I better go. I have to meet my dad at senior barn."

"Okay, Lyn, I'll talk to you tomorrow." Amanda stood and watched me say good-bye yet again to my old horse. She put her arm around me as we walked down the hill towards senior barn.

"Make sure you find me tomorrow, Okay?" She asked. I assured her that I would and walked to senior barn where my Dad was already waiting.

I told him the price for Nejaunee and the look of disappointment showed on his face. I knew he felt bad about it, I also knew what he would say.

"I'm sorry, honey. We could never come up with that much money," he said.

"I know, Dad." I turned towards the window and we rode home in silence. There was nothing he could say. I went in the house and up to my room. I didn't come down until morning.

The next morning was cold and rainy. I ate my breakfast and rode silently to camp. My Dad told me how terrible he and Mom felt about the horse,

49

but they didn't have six hundred dollars to lend to me. I knew they couldn't help me.

I got out of the car at senior barn and helped feed and water the horses. Most of the campers had already gone home and the rest were leaving today. I finished quickly at the barn and headed to Lee's cabin. Lee was leaving today as well.

"Knock, knock," I said as I rapped on the cabin door.

"C'mon in!" Lee yelled to me.

"All packed and ready?" I asked trying to sound cheerful.

"As ready as I'll ever be," Lee responded. We talked about arrangements for her visit at Christmastime.

"Another summer gone. It's hard to believe it's almost September," Lee said. "Oh, by the way, Amanda was looking for you."

"Okay, I'll find her later."

"You know, Lyn, you did all that you could to save that mare. I can't believe what a jerk Tim has been, but you have to look at it this way: You gave that horse six months of love and good care. Care that she would not have had if you hadn't been involved. You have to believe that."

"I know. I'm going to see if she's even still there. I dread that climb up the hill to the pasture. I'm afraid of what I'll see, or rather, what I won't see."

Lee hugged me and we picked up her bags and carried them to the van that would take her to the airport.

"Keep me informed. Call if you need to, I'm always there for you. I'll be thinking of the two of you," Lee told me as she got into the van. I watched her drive away and thought, not a better friend could be found.

I took a deep breath and walked to junior barn. By the time that I reached the pasture, my legs were soaked from the wet grass. I looked across the pasture searching for the horses. Panic flooded over me. I couldn't find them!

"Nejaunee!" I yelled, running to the fence. A startled Nejaunee threw her head up and snorted.

"Oh, thank God," I whispered when I saw her. As I searched the pasture, I realized that my little horse was alone. I walked along the fence wondering; hoping the colt had escaped. Surely, they wouldn't have taken him to slaughter and left Nejaunee. The fence was secure; there was no escaped horse. As I walked to the barn I could see tire tracks in the mud. I could see where the trailer had been and the scrambled hoof prints where the colt had refused to load. Was he a bad loader or did he know where he was headed? I shuddered. Why had they left Nejaunee? Couldn't they get her loaded? No, that couldn't be it. Two men could have almost picked her up and loaded her. She wasn't a fighter. I had more questions than I had answers, but I had to believe that this was a good sign.

I had to find Tim, as much as I hated seeing him, I knew he would have the answers. No wait, Amanda might know. I went there first.

I walked to Amanda's cabin and knocked on the door.

"Come in please," Amanda called.

"Hi, Amanda, it's me, Lyn," I called back. "Do you know if they took that Thoroughbred colt to the auction? He's not in the pasture, but Nauj is still there."

Amanda entered the front room brushing her hair.

"I'm sorry, Lyn, yes he's gone. I know it doesn't seem right just to dispose of them like that".

"It would be kinder to just put him down," I mumbled.

"I agree with you, but Tim would never pass up money to do what is right."

"Why didn't they take Nejaunee?" I asked trying to hide the hope that I felt.

"I talked to Tim, I told him to leave you alone and give you that horse at no charge," Amanda said hiding any emotion.

I stared at her, processing what she said.

"You mean I can have her! Nejaunee's mine?" I shouted at her.

"All you have to do is find a place to keep her. Tim will take care of her until you do. I wouldn't put it off, though." Her smile was as broad as mine was.

"I can never thank you enough. You'll never know how much this means to me. This is the nicest thing anyone has ever done for me!" I told her.

"You're not out of the forest yet. You have to find a stable and you have to get her there," Amanda reminded me.

"I have a stable! I'll walk her there if I have to!" I assured her. I hugged her and ran to junior barn to tell Nauj.

That afternoon I told my father the good news.

"That's wonderful!" he exclaimed. Then we discussed once more all that was required to keep and care for her. I know he was a little afraid that we had forgotten something, but I had gone over it so many times that I was certain it would all work out.

That night I called Mrs. Moore to make sure that the offer still stood. Everything was in place. I called a couple different horse-trucking companies and was shocked at the cost of trailering my horse twelve miles. I couldn't afford it. Undeterred I told my dad that I would walk her home. At first, my parents weren't thrilled with the idea, but they knew I was too determined to be swayed.

"I'll walk her on the shoulder of the road. We'll be fine," I told them. I didn't think that she would be able to carry me twelve miles, I had no saddle or bridle and I didn't know how she was in traffic, but I figured we could walk on the shoulder no problem. All I had to do was finalize the plans.

CHAPTER 7

The planning took longer than I had expected. I continued to work at camp but only to keep an eye on Nejaunee. I was afraid if I wasn't there, Tim would get rid of her now that Amanda had gone home. I trusted him less with each passing day and fears of what he might do lie in my stomach like a stone every night.

Mrs. Moore wasn't able to guarantee an empty stall until late in October. I sweated it out for two months at camp before I was able to plan our departure. I informed Tim that I would be leaving with Nejaunee the next Saturday. He didn't say much and I didn't know how to take him. I was only fourteen and still didn't understand everything adults did. I couldn't figure out why he let me stay and work and care for my horse. I figured either he wasn't as bad a person as I thought, or more likely, Amanda really had some authority over him.

Saturday morning broke cold but clear. The sun shone as if it was happy. I had breakfast with my parents and my brother and even though they were still a bit apprehensive about horse ownership, I knew they were happy for me, too. John and I made the drive to camp one more time. The plan was that he would periodically check on me as I walked along the roadway. I felt a bit of nostalgia as we drove the length of the driveway to senior barn. I knew that this would be my last trip to camp and through it all, I still had a lot of good memories. I looked out at the pasture full of camp horses that didn't find winter homes. I knew all of them by name and I realized just how much I would miss them. I felt a pang of sadness at the thought of never seeing them again. I silently asked God to look after them. I wished I could take them all home.

John pulled up to the barn and parked next to Tim's truck. I took a deep breath and got out. I couldn't understand why he intimidated me so. My palms were sweating and my heart pounding as I went into the barn. I still feared that he would change his mind and she'd be gone, Amanda or no Amanda. I was glad John was with me, but he looked a little apprehensive himself. He wouldn't let Tim get stupid or anything, but ultimately, Tim still held all the cards. He still owned Nejaunee and could do with her as he pleased. Tim had been mean in the past, I didn't quite believe he wouldn't be again. I imagined his glee in telling me," Sorry, I changed my mind, I sent your horse to slaughter this morning". The thought made me shudder. I tried to shake off the dreadful feeling as I walked into the barn.

Tim barely acknowledged me as he took the halter and lead line from me. He entered a stall and led Nejaunee into the aisle.

He turned to me and said," you need to give me a dollar bill to make the sale legal."

I reached into my pocket and removed a dollar. I carefully smoothed it out and handed it to him. He took the bill, handed the lead line to me and said flatly," I'm cheating you, this horse isn't worth a dollar."

I took the lead, trying to conceal the nervous shake in my hands and with all the courage I could muster, snapped at him," I 'm stealing her from you, she's worth a lot more than that!" I surprised myself with the venomous tone of my voice. I suddenly felt very protective of my horse and myself. He no longer had control over me or her and all the times he had held her life or death over me as a way of manipulating me were gone. The intimidation I had felt turned to rage. It was the first time that I had stood up to an adult. My brother looked a little shocked but said nothing. I gave Nejaunee a pat on the neck and walked out. I didn't even look back at Tim. I no longer cared what he was going to do.

John got into his truck." Okay, you ready?"

"Yeah, go ahead. I'll be okay.

"I'll follow you for a while, that way you'll be safe."

I walked down the driveway with my horse. *My* horse. I felt an incredible rush of freedom, as if I had been released from some terrible prison. As we walked past the other horses they slowly raised their heads to look at us. "Sorry guys, I wish you could come too", I whispered to them. *You can't save them all.* Well, maybe not, but hadn't any of those people ever heard the story about the starfish on the beach? The one that goes, there's two people walking on a beach when one reaches down and picks up a stranded starfish and puts it back into the water. The other person says," You can't save the world."

"I know", replies the other, "but I just saved *his* world."

Nejaunee and I stopped at the end of the drive. We both turned to take one last look. She seemed to understand the importance of the moment. I felt that a period in my life was ending and a new one was beginning. In all the mix of emotion, all I could say was "good riddance", and we turned and walked out onto the road.

John followed directly behind us with his flashers on for quite a while. As the cars passed they would slow down to see what he was doing and when they saw me, would shake their heads in disbelief. I must have been quite a sight.

As I walked down the road I thought a lot about all that had happened. It had been rough, but in the end it had all been worth it. This one little horse that I *could* save would never know another hungry day or cold night. I knew at her advanced age that we wouldn't have a lot of time together, but I vowed right then that her remaining years would be as happy and as comfortable as I could make them. After all she'd been through she deserved that much.

As we reached David road I stopped and waited for John to pull alongside. "I'm okay, the traffic's pretty light today".

"Okay, I'll be back in a little while to check on you." He waved as he pulled away and Nejaunee and I crossed the street and headed up David Road. The wind was now in our faces and I put my hood up and walked backwards for a while. The wind was blowing Nejaunee's mane and making her eyes water. The expression on her face was of mild curiosity. Another adventure I guess. "How many adventures have you had, ol' girl?" Plenty I'll bet. What a remarkable animal she was. She had been mistreated several times, maybe many more than I knew of, yet here she was, walking with me and trusting me with whatever we were about to do. I don't know if animals are capable of forgiveness, but certainly this mare had every reason to be mistrustful of people. She walked the entire way with that sweet, curious expression of hers. It was many years and many horses later before I realized just how special this horse was.

The traffic didn't seem to bother her at all. I guess she'll be road safe, I thought. At that point I was wishing that I could have ridden her a little ways. My foot was beginning to hurt and I still had a long way to go. Twelve miles was farther than I thought. If I had owned a bridle I could have at least ridden a little of the way bareback. All I had for her were a few brushes and a halter and lead rope. I didn't own a saddle or a bridle, but at this point that didn't matter.

John came by a few times and brought me some water. The wind was cold, but the sun came out a little and I began to feel a little better. When we turned onto Strong Road I knew we only had a couple more miles to go. "Not much farther now, girl", I told her and wondered if her legs were aching as much as mine. I tried to forget the ache in my legs by thinking of all the fun things we would do. I was proud of myself for what I had done to make Nejaunee my own. It was a time in my life that finding pride in myself was difficult, to say the least. Being a teenager was difficult and many times I didn't feel like I did anything right. I knew, no matter what anyone else thought; that what I was doing now was the right thing to do.

The trees that grew along the road were quite large and most of the leaves were already gone. The weatherman was predicting an early winter and at that moment I believed him. I briefly closed my eyes trying to memorize this day. I knew it was important to remember this first day of horse ownership. When I opened my eyes, I could just make out the roof of the barn. The excitement I felt made me break into a jog and Nauj trotted diligently behind me.

John pulled up just as we approached the driveway to the barn. He followed us until we were safely in the driveway, then he pulled up by the house and got out of the truck. "Well, you made it".

"Yeah, my legs are killing me, but we're here. Here, hold her while I go get Mrs. Moore".

"Hold her? I don't know how to hold her", he said.

I laughed out loud, "Just hold the rope, she's not going to do anything". I handed him the lead rope and walked away. When I looked back, he was looking rather apprehensively at her. Nejaunee just stood there and yawned.

Mrs. Moore opened the door when she saw me and said" Go in that back barn there, I think there are some empty stalls in there." I thanked her and walked back to where John was standing.

"Do you need a ride home?"

"Um, yeah. Could you have Dad come and get me around four?"

"Okay. See you later", he said as he got into the truck.

"Hey, John. Thanks. For everything." He just nodded back to me, but I knew he understood how much I meant it.

I led Nejaunee to the courtyard entrance of the barn and through the door. The courtyard was a concrete area that separated two barns. There was a huge sliding door that separated the courtyard from the driveway. It was too heavy to push open, so we walked through the person door. I could see the horses turned out in the pasture and there were horses in the big barn, but I didn't see any people. Mrs. Moore had said that she was leasing the barn to a trainer and there were several people boarding their horses there. I was anxious to meet the owners and trainer. I wanted to learn all that I could and what a wealth of knowledge a trainer would be. I led Nauj into the small barn that Mrs. Moore had pointed out. I figured I'd get her settled before Dad came back for me. I put her on the crossties and looked at the stalls. There were no horses in the barn, but all of the stalls were dirty. The barn was a lean-to and the stalls were small and had dirt floors. The stalls were poorly built, but Nejaunee was good in her stall and most importantly, she had shelter.

I found a pitchfork and a wheelbarrow and went to work cleaning one of the stalls. While I worked I couldn't help but feel happy. Nejaunee was mine now. She was safe and I had fulfilled a life-long dream of owning my own horse. I didn't even mind cleaning the stalls.

As I finished cleaning the stall, a woman stepped into the barn.

"What are you doing?" she demanded. I straightened up and said, "Hi, I'm Lyn. Mrs. Moore told me that I could put my horse in one of these stalls. If this one is taken, I can clean out another one."

"They're all taken," she snapped back. Then she turned her attention to Nejaunee. With her hands on her hips she looked her up and down. I glowed with pride and happiness; Nejaunee looked beautiful to me. She was still a bit thin, but her coat shone like a copper penny and her eyes were as bright as a small child's on Christmas morning. She stood with one hind leg resting on its toe and gently swished her tail. She was the picture of contentment and even a novice like myself could see the fine temperament and sensibility she possessed. I loved her.

"Where did you get this horse?"

"I bought her from a camp for a dollar. She was on her way to the slaughter house", I said with pride.

"You paid a dollar for this horse?" It was more of a statement than a question.

"Yes", I answered more hesitantly.

"You got cheated," she laughed, "you should have let her go for dog food." Then she turned to me and said, "She can't stay in here, there's no stall available. She'll have to stay outside. Mrs. Moore doesn't run this barn, I do. Don't forget that. I hope she's had her shots, you know I have a lot of valuable horses here."

I felt the burn of tears and willed them away. I did not want to cry in front of this woman. I wondered briefly if she could be related to Tim.

"She's had her shots. Are you Carol?" I asked, knowing the answer.

"Yes I am. I hope you have your own supplies. I don't know what arrangement you made with Mrs. Moore, but I'm not feeding that animal."

"I have my own stuff, I just need somewhere to put it."

"You can put your feed over in that corner, no one will touch it." Carol turned and walked out.

I just stood there for a minute wondering what to do next. I wanted to turn the wheelbarrow over into the stall I had just cleaned, but then thought better of it. I emptied the wheelbarrow on the manure pile and returned to the barn. I cleaned out the corner as best as I could. I could see where the roof had leaked and washed some of the floor away. I spent the rest of the day grooming and grazing Nejaunee. I wasn't going to let Carol ruin my day.

Dad pulled in at four and had brought the feed and hay we bought the week before. He helped me carry my grain, hay, brushes and buckets to my corner. Dad had brought a clean garbage can to put the feed in. When we poured the grain into it, Nejaunee nickered at the sound. I poured a scoop of grain into a feed pan for her. I unsnapped the crossties and held the lead while she ate. My Dad commented on how she cleaned up every last bit. I walked her out of the barn and waited until Carol had brought in all of the other horses. Nejaunee would be outside by herself, but she had a large run-in shed in the big barn and could see the other horses from there. At least no one would bully her out of her food. I put a couple of flakes of hay and a bucket of water in the shed for her. I kissed her as she quietly munched her hay. I took her halter off and walked out to the courtyard where my Dad was waiting.

"This sure is a beautiful old barn," he said. I would hear him say that more than a few times.

I could see Nauj eating her hay in the run-in shed. She wasn't the least bit concerned that she didn't have a stall. Maybe this wouldn't be so bad after all. I decided not to mention the stall to my Dad. I didn't want anything to go wrong. If Mrs. Moore expected me to work to pay for a stall, I would just do it. There was no reason to mention it, what if she decided I couldn't stay? Obviously, she didn't know what was going on in the barn. Carol was probably lying about how many horses she had there. My telling would jam me up for sure. I'd be invisible to Carol and friendly and helpful to everyone else. I had to make this work.

I walked to the car with Dad while he told me about how this barn was a spectacular beef cattle farm when they had first moved to town. As I sat in the car, I realized just how tired I was. I took one last look at the barn and smiled. I was pleased, in spite of the little set back with Carol. "Sleep well, sweetie", I whispered as we pulled onto the road and headed home.

CHAPTER 8

As soon as I got home from church the next morning, I changed into my jeans and rode my bike to the barn. It was little warmer and the barn was only a mile from home, so it was an easy ride. I walked out to the pasture and called her name. Nejaunee looked up and walked over to greet me. I put her halter on and led her to the barn. I filled her feed tub and let her eat. There were other horses out with her now, but it appeared that they had left her alone. The pasture was pretty big and she had lots of room to avoid aggressive horses if she had to. When she finished her meal, I led her to the pasture fence and tied her to the post. I figured that I wouldn't be in anyone's way there. She stood quietly while I gave her a thorough grooming.

I heard a car pull up to the barn and braced myself for Carol. Maybe she'd just ignore me. A few minutes later a woman of about forty with dark hair walked towards me carrying a halter. "Hi, I'm Joan", she said. "I own Sunny, that big chestnut over there," she said pointing to a large Thoroughbred with a pretty head.

"I'm Lyn", I said politely. "She's really pretty", I added as I admired her horse.

"You bought this mare off of the meat wagon?" she asked.

"Yeah", was all I offered. I didn't want to hear how I had gotten cheated.

"What a nice thing to do. She seems very sweet. How old is she?"

I was relieved at her kindness. I was weary from defending my actions. "Well, the vet's not sure of her age. They say after twenty it's hard to tell, but he figures upper twenties."

"Wow. Well she looks as though she's on the road to better health now, doesn't she?"

"Yeah, she was starved a long time. I guess it's hard to recover from that when they're so old".

"Seems to have a little Morgan in her, doesn't she? "she asked, not waiting for a response. She smiled brightly and went to catch her horse. I was grateful for the kind words.

In the weeks and months that followed I got to know Joan and the other boarders well. Some I liked better than others, but they were all pretty nice to me. Joan loaned me an old bridle and I rode across half the county bareback. I could ride Nauj to my house and tie her in the yard while I ate lunch. This habit led to an 'investigation' by the local police on a complaint that we were housing horses in my father's tractor shed. I think the officer was disappointed to find only the lawn tractor and assorted tools there.

The fall was a beautiful time to ride. Nejaunee and I rode through the woods and fields and enjoyed the change of colors and the activity of all the animal life. I felt so free and completely at ease during those rides. She was a wonderful trail horse and went anywhere that I pointed her. Out in the woods it was just the two of us. I would talk while she would listen. Sometimes, we would come upon other people walking or picnicking. I always enjoyed the look of surprise on their faces when we walked up on them.

Every night I would wait until Carol's horses were in so that I could leave Nauj her hay for the evening. Then I would ride my bike home. I stayed away from Carol and she ignored me. I thought that was just fine.

Shortly before Christmas I received an early present. Carol loaded up her horses and moved them to another barn. Nejaunee had a stall for the winter and the atmosphere at the barn changed dramatically. Everyone was relieved. The boarders that had horses in training with Carol left with her, of course, so the rest of us "back-yarders" had the place to ourselves. After Carol left Mrs. Moore needed someone to feed the horses every morning and evening. That became an integral part of my job. I was the new barn manager and I tried to do my best. Each boarder was responsible for supplying their own feed, hay and bedding and for cleaning their horse's stall. I attended the same high school where my father was a teacher, so he drove me to the barn every day before and after school to feed the horses. It meant that we had to leave earlier in the mornings to get to school on time, but Dad seemed to almost enjoy it. We would feed, water and hay the horses that stayed in and set out hay and water for the horses we turned out. In the evening we would bring the horses in and repeat the feeding. I was grateful for all the help and support that I got from my family. There were times that they helped me load hay into the mow or shovel snow or carry feed or whatever needed doing. My parents helped out financially when I didn't have enough to cover my feed bills and they and my brother constantly taxied me to and from the barn. I knew that I could never repay them.

Christmas morning I woke to find a brand new saddle, bridle and saddle pad waiting under the tree. After we opened all of our gifts and had our traditional homemade cinnamon roll, I put on my snowsuit and begged for a ride to the barn.

"You're going to ride on Christmas day?" my Mom asked.

"Mom, we have to feed the horses and clean her stall anyway. Besides no one else will be over until this afternoon and we went to church last night. Please, Mom."

"Oh, okay. I guess it won't matter if you're there for a little while." I had a new saddle and bridle what did she expect me to do?

I grabbed Nejaunee's stocking that was filled with her favorite treats, (after-dinner mints) and the bridle and John took my saddle and we were out the door. The streets were deserted and the town had a warm peaceful look to it. John dropped me off and told me to call when I was ready to come home.

The horses nickered when I went into the barn. Anxious for their breakfast, I was always a welcome sight. I fed them and turned them out. I put hay out and spread it out so that they all could get some. I had to break the ice out of the water tank but I didn't have to fill it. I went into the tack room and got my brushes to groom Nauj. She stood quietly while I brushed her and fed her a few treats. I talked to her constantly although she had yet to answer. Maybe it was better that way. I put on her new pad and carefully lowered the saddle to her back. The pad was a good thick one and it protected her back well. The saddle fit well and cleared her high withers. I had been worried that her sway back and fallen off top line would create a fit problem. I fastened the cinch gently and then stretched her front legs out to free any pinched skin under the cinch. At her age the skin on her underside sagged and caused her pain if it got trapped under the cinch. I bridled her and stepped back. She looked beautiful in her new tack. Just like a little cow-pony should.

We went through the gate into the freezing air. I pulled my collar up and tightened the cinch. I adjusted the stirrups and mounted up. The saddle felt so different than riding bareback. It felt like she was so far away from me. I couldn't feel her sides or the warmth of her body. I knew that I would miss riding bareback, but I also believed that the saddle was probably more comfortable for her and I knew I'd get used to it. At least I wouldn't get so much horsehair on my jeans.

I could see her breath as we made our way up the hill behind the barn and into the field. The saddle creaked with every step she took and it smelled delightfully of the tack shop. It was a crisp, beautiful day and the sun made the ice on the trees sparkle and glisten. It was so quiet I felt like I was in the middle of Montana instead of upstate New York. Nejaunee was always an energetic ride and she felt especially frisky in the cold. She plowed right through the high drifts of snow and pranced when we entered a small patch of evergreens. Inside the trees there was no wind, no sound and very little snow. When we stopped I could hear the chatter of squirrels who voiced their anger at our intrusion. I closed my eyes. Thank you, God, I whispered. If I die today I'll have died happy. Thank you for giving me this horse and this quiet place to enjoy. This is what horses did best. People showed them, worked them, sold them, "owned" them, but this was the true gift. The peace and solitude and pure beauty of them are what make us love them so much. The ride back to the barn was wonderful. We loped through the field back to the barn, breaking through the snowdrifts that rose to Nejaunee's chest. I think she enjoyed it as much as I did. When I sighted the barn I made her walk so that she would be cool by the time we got there. It was a very memorable Christmas. It was days like this that helped me endure the difficult times the teen-age years brought. Whenever I was sad or confused I always went to the barn and it always cheered me up. I had friends that had tried drugs or alcohol, looking for what they couldn't find. Looking for what I had. I know that now, I knew it then. I was lucky. I was blessed. This skinny little horse had given me a gift that would long outlive her. She had given me a passion that would sustain and nurture me throughout my life. One that would bring me great joy and even great sadness, but it helped shape the identity of the person I was then and the one I am today.

CHAPTER 9

The next month proved quite eventful for our area. Dubbed the Blizzard of '77 by the media, western New York received several feet of snow in a matter of hours. High winds created below zero wind chills and life threatening conditions. Schools and businesses were closed. There was a driving ban issued, which made it illegal to be on the roads. People froze to death in their cars and homes. It was the first time that I ever thought about snow as more than something to sled on.

"Dad, How are we going to feed the horses?" I asked very concerned.

"I don't know. We can't drive to the barn. They won't survive very long without water." I knew Mrs. Moore wouldn't know what to do and none of the other boarders lived nearby.

"We could go on the snowmobile", John offered.

"Yes! That's it! Let's go!" I yelled running for my snowsuit.

So John drove the snowmobile the mile to the barn. At first we went through the fields, but we realized that due to the driving ban there were no cars on the road so we drove right down the middle of the road.

The snow had drifted in front of the barn door and it took us a little while to dig it out. When we got inside the horses were quite upset at how late we were. We fed them and put them out. We opened a bale of hay in the run-in shed and the horses never left it. The snow was so deep; they couldn't get out of the run in. We cleaned the stalls and broke the ice out of the buckets. When we tried to fill them, however, the pipes had frozen and no water came out. We hauled water from Mrs. Moore's house to fill the buckets and the trough. By the time we were done we were exhausted. I was grateful for all the help. I could never have done it alone. That evening we rode back down and brought them in and fed them. Every day that was our routine for the next several days. I had used my Christmas money to buy Nauj a blanket and was glad I had, in light of all the sub-freezing nights.

When spring finally arrived I think everyone breathed a sigh of relief. As the days got longer and warmer the horses began to shed their long winter coats. Nejaunee was slower shedding out than the others because of her advanced age, but she looked good and had held her weight. I knew she would never be fat, but she had muscled up and only a glint of her ribs showed now. By May her coat was slick and the new grass put the finishing touches on her over-all health. She looked better than I had ever seen her.

On school days Dad and I continued to drive to the barn to do morning chores. Every once in a while, on a beautiful spring morning, I would beg him to let me stay at the barn and skip school. It must have been hard for him to allow it, but sometimes he would give in to my need for a 'mental health day'.

Summer created new problems for Nejaunee and I worked endlessly trying to keep the flies off of her. There were not a lot of fly control products available then and my little mare suffered. Her eyes drooped where the flies fed in them and her skin had welts all over from bites. I kept her in during the heat of the day and tried every product available. I tied strips of bed sheet to her halter to keep the flies off her face. Her belly was the worst. The skin there sagged and the flies feasted on her. She never stood head to tail like the other horses, she was always by herself and she didn't have the energy to swat at the flies all day long. Dr. James advised me to smear diaper ointment on her belly to discourage the flies. It actually worked quite well, although people often wondered why the barn smelled like a nursery.

Over the next few months Nejaunee continued to thrive. I tried every new supplement that promised weight gain and followed Dr. James advice religiously. Some of my friends from school purchased horses and boarded them at Mrs. Moore's. I continued to care for the horses as part of my board and I took a part-time job painting jump standards for a man who supplied the fences for hunter/jumper shows. I worked nights at a local tack shop and learned a lot about horse equipment. Best of all, I got fifteen percent off any purchase at the store.

My friends with horses didn't have to work to support them, but that never bothered me. They had expensive equipment and registered, well-broke horses. After we rode, they would go home and I would have to stay to mow the lawn or trim the hedges or paint something. Sometimes they made fun of me a little bit, but it was a small price to pay for the privilege of horse ownership.

My Dad purchased an old horse trailer and the entire family sanded and repainted it. That summer I hauled Nejaunee to several local horse shows. We competed in the game classes and even won a few ribbons. Nejaunee always gave all she had for me. More than once, I was approached by the show stewards over Nejaunee's condition. I told my story over and over. Once they realized her age and her previous condition, they were very supportive. At the age of fifteen I didn't realize that I should not have been competing with her, but she didn't seem to realize it either. I took her to the Erie County Fair in Hamburg, New York that year. The fair was huge and most of the horse show was A rated. Some of the finest horses and riders in the area were there. I showed in the un-rated games classes, but it was still a big event. Nejaunee and I won fourth place in the can race that year. The can race was my favorite. There were three barrels set in the arena in the cloverleaf barrel race pattern, but instead of turning around them, you had to run on the outside of them and knock a pop can off each barrel. The horse and rider who knocked all of the cans off in the fastest time won. Some of the horses would set up and veer away at the barrels, afraid of the cans that flew out in front of them. Nejaunee never wavered; she just lowered her head and ran as fast as I asked her to. The horsemen watching told me she had a lot of heart. I knew that she always gave one hundred percent, I was glad that others saw it too.

I continued to ride and show Nejaunee for two more years before she started to slow down. I knew her age was finally catching up to her and decided it was time to let her retire. I still rode her occasionally on an easy trail ride and cared for her diligently, but I let her spend most of her days out in the pasture. That meant that I would need another horse. I was working steady and would be able to support two horses. That August I called Tim to see if I could take Grey Knight for the winter. Surprisingly, he no longer frightened me. I took Grey Knight and my best friend, Kelly, took a camp horse also. The two of us had a great time that year. We were inseparable. We spent most of our schooldays together and the rest of the evening riding and caring for our horses. I couldn't have asked for anything else. Especially since Lee's visits were becoming fewer and fewer. I knew that we were growing up and heading our own ways. Still, I missed her terribly and it was great to have someone to pal around with at the barn.

One fall day I was riding Grey Knight and decided to jump him over a few fences, like the old days at camp. I set the fences at three foot, six inches, a comfortable height for him. I put on my hard hat and climbed on bareback. I warmed him up and cantered him around the small course I had set up. After a couple of trips around, I dismounted and raised one of the fences to 3"9". When he cleared that easily, I raised it again, this time to 4'. That is a good-sized fence for an old camp horse like Grey Knight and too high for an inexperienced rider mounted bareback, no less. As we approached the jump, I knew the distance was wrong. My inexperience left me wondering whether I should speed him up to extend his stride or hold him and take an extra stride. My indecision left Grey Knight to decide for himself. He couldn't meet the fence properly, so he took an extra small stride, which placed him too close to the fence for a proper take-off. I thought he was going to refuse and stop, but he tried to jump it anyway. He had come to an almost complete stop before he jumped and the momentum carried me over his head. I landed on the other side of the fence and turned in time to see his front feet coming at me. I rolled sideways hoping to avoid being struck upon his landing. He tried to avoid me by separating his feet. This left him without much support base and he crashed to the ground in front of me. I turned to look at him and felt a sharp pain across my back and my head ached. He had partially landed on my head. He got to his feet and looked at me. I could see there was blood on his nose from a scratch on his upper lip, otherwise he appeared fine. I slowly got to my feet and walked to him. I felt a little dizzy, but I led the horse to the barn, checked him over and put him away. I didn't feel as though I could ride my bike home so Mrs. Moore drove me there. I walked into my living room and grabbed onto the archway as the room began to spin. My brother helped me to the couch and asked me what happened. After I told him, he brought me an ice pack for my now throbbing head and telephoned for an ambulance. As the world spun around me, I fought to remain conscious. My parents arrived home and I recall hearing my mother say" I knew this would happen."

I ended up with a mild concussion and an extreme headache. My hard hat had probably saved my life. Hard hats are not like the helmets of today. All they were was a steel shell with a little bit of foam on the inside. Grey Knight's hoof print was clearly imbedded in the velvet covering. He had landed his right front foot directly on my skull. I had learned my lesson, no more jumping until I had proper instruction.

When I returned Grey Knight to camp that summer, I realized that I needed my own horse. My parents agreed and I borrowed the money from my grandparents. I found a two-year-old Appaloosa mare named Gypsy. I bought her and trained her myself. I realize now that the only reason I succeeded with her training is because she was such a nice mare. She was extremely affectionate and loved attention. Whenever she saw me walk into the barn she would trot up to the gate and wait for me. Gypsy grew into a large, muscular horse and she was fun to ride. She had a quiet and sensible demeanor and was well suited for the western pleasure classes that I wanted to try.

I would soon be graduating from high school and began to consider what I would do with my life. I wanted to attend Veterinary school or become a horse trainer. My parents worried that I did not have the grades or money to attend vet school and trainers had to be world class in order succeed. Unsure of what to do, I attended a local college and worked full time to support my horse habit.

By 1981 I owned four horses and boarded them all at Mrs. Moore's. The barn was not being kept up and the pasture and fences were deteriorating, but I could not afford to move them all. The horses came in at night with their manes and tails matted with burdocks. Nejaunee was having trouble keeping weight on and was really showing her age. We believed her to be over thirty now. Her molars were almost completely gone now which made chewing difficult. I ground up her grain and mixed it with beetpulp soaked in water. She began to quid her hay and would chew it and spit it out, unable to chew it enough to swallow it. I bought the finest clover hay that I could find and wet it to make it more palatable. By fall of that year, Nejaunee was losing weight and was wearing two blankets. Her appearance suffered, but she was still energetic and seemed pain-free and content.

CHAPTER 10

In January of 1982 I was working at a local store while I pursued a career in law enforcement. I was working several menial jobs in order to support my growing horse habit.

On January third I received a call at work from a friend at the barn.

"You'd better come quick," Kathy told me. "Nejaunee's fallen down in the pasture and I can't get her up!"

I told my employer that I had a family emergency and sped to the barn. I ran into the pasture where Kathy was squatting next to my downed horse.

"I can't get her up. I think she slipped on the ice."

I kneeled next to Nauj's head. "Easy, girl. What happened to you?" I said gently. I took a hold of her halter and gently pulled, urging her to her feet. She made no effort to rise. I could tell from the marks in the snow that she had struggled to get up until she exhausted herself. Kathy and I grabbed her tail and tried to pull her rump off of the ice. Nejaunee just looked confused and made no effort to get up. Then I took a hold of her neck and Kathy pushed on her hip until we were able to roll her up on her chest. While I pulled on her halter, Kathy pulled on her tail until Nejaunee

83

finally heaved herself to her feet. She stood splay-legged and trembling. I didn't know if she was fatigued or just frightened. She was wet and cold and Kathy and I slowly walked her into the barn. I took off her wet blanket and put on a dry one. I looked her over and could find no swelling or injury.

"She must have slipped and couldn't get her footing on the ice," Kathy said.

"Yeah…then she must have struggled until she was exhausted," I added. I put her in her stall and stayed with her a while. She seemed to have forgotten the whole ordeal and quietly munched on her hay. I stayed at the barn until evening. Then I did the evening chores and checked Nauj one more time. I went home to supper and returned that evening for one last check. She blinked curiously at me in the bright light when I turned on the aisle lights. All was well, so I went home to bed.

The next morning I went in to feed as usual. When I entered the barn, I couldn't see Nejaunee above the boards of her stall. I heard banging and thrashing as I ran to her stall. She was down and cast in her stall. She was facing the wall, her knees pressed against it. She must have rolled over, and with her knees against the boards, did not have the room to get her feet underneath her. I went to her head and tried to comfort her. "Easy girl, it's okay now. I'll get you up." She looked at me in complete hopelessness, her eyes wide with fear. I pulled on her tail trying to move her away from the wall. The wooden floor was wet with urine and water from her bucket that had been knocked off its' hook. I slipped and fell next to her. I couldn't budge her. I felt tears well up in my eyes as I began to wonder if this was more than exhaustion from her fall on the ice. I went to her head and placed it in my lap. I stroked her neck and spoke soothingly to her. She relaxed and her breathing slowed. Her look of panic slowly became one of 'what now?' I gently lowered her head to the hay and ran to call my father.

"Dad? Nejaunee's down again. I can't get her up. Could you come and help me?"

When my father arrived, we went to her stall and pulled her away from the wall. We pushed and pulled until we got her on her feet. I put Nejaunee in the run in shed and closed the door. If she went down at least she wouldn't get cast in there. I called Dr. James and waited for his arrival.

When the vet arrived, I led Nauj into the barn where he could examine her. Dr. James listened to her heart and lungs and he drew a sample of blood.

"You know, Lyn," he began gently, "You have done wonders with this horse, but you have to realize that she is well past her life expectancy. You may have to consider how long she has left. Horses never seem to do us the favor, usually they make us make the decision for them." I knew what he was talking about. Euthanasia.

"I know, Doc, but she seems better. Maybe she just got exhausted from struggling."

"Maybe. I'll run some tests. I'll call you tomorrow with the results. I put Nauj back into the run in shed and gave her some hay.

I took the rest of the day off from work and stayed at the barn. The weather was extremely cold. I put both blankets on Nejaunee and brought warm water for her to drink. I spent the night on the living room couch thinking about what Dr. James had said. I checked on Nejaunee frequently throughout the night. I could see that she was getting weaker. I didn't want to face it, but Nejaunee was in failing health. I hoped that she was merely exhausted, but I feared that it was more than that.

In the morning I fed the horses and watched Nejaunee eat her grain. She ate with vigor, but she seemed tired. Really tired. I brushed her and rubbed all of her favorite spots. The blankets were made of wool and canvas and they were heavy, but it was so cold I decided to put them back on her. I went home to wait for Dr. James to call.

"Hello?" I said when the phone rang.

"Lyn? This is Dr. James. I got those results back…" My throat closed as his words trailed off. "Lyn, Nejaunee is an old horse. Horses aren't meant to live this long. This horse suffered through severe starvation. Sometimes their organs never fully recover…You gave this horse six wonderful years…Lyn, Nejaunee's kidneys have stopped functioning…She's going to die. If you don't put her to sleep, she'll suffer until she dies. I know how hard this is, but it's time to do the right thing…for her. You gave her six years she would have never had. With out you, she would have been sold and slaughtered. I know you love her, but you have to make the decision to put her down. You have to love her enough to help her now."

I couldn't speak. I choked on my tears. The silence on the phone was deafening.

"Lyn? I'm sorry, I wish I had better news."

I regained some control, "Dr. James, what time frame are we talking about?"

"I wouldn't wait too long, we don't want her to suffer. A day or two at the most."

"Okay. I'll have to find a place to bury her." It seemed a strange comment, but suddenly very important.

I went downstairs with my tragic news and explained Nejaunee's condition as well as I could to my Mom and Dad. Through tears I told them I wanted to bury her.

"The town won't allow you to bury her, honey, it's against the law."

"I know, Dad. I was thinking of that pet cemetery."

"Oh boy, I think it might be very expensive to bury a horse there. Why don't we call the renderers to come and get her."

I burst out in uncontrollable tears. I had cried so much I couldn't have stopped now if I wanted to. "No Dad, please! I know it doesn't make sense to you, but the thought of it is unbearable to me. I'll pay whatever it costs to bury her. I'll borrow it if I have to. Please, I worked so hard to keep her from that fate it just doesn't seem right."

"Okay, go call them and see what it will cost. I just don't see the reason when someone will pay us for her carcass. She'll be dead you know." I didn't answer. What was the point? My father would never understand how I felt. I knew though that he would help me to bury her because he loved me, even if he never understood it all.

After making arrangements with the cemetery, I called Dr. James. We agreed to meet at the cemetery the next morning.

"What if she goes down in the trailer?" I asked him.

"We'll put her to sleep in the trailer and then pull her body out."

It all seemed so surreal. I was making the necessary plans as if it was for something else. It never all connected in my mind what we were about to do.

At ten o'clock that night I pulled on my winter boots and snowsuit.

"Are you sure you're going to be all right? It's below zero out there"; my Mom said twisting her dishtowel in her hands.

"I'll be okay. If I get too cold I'll sit in the car for a while", I sighed. I picked up the blanket and the thermos of hot chocolate and stepped out into the frigid night air. I planned on spending the night in the barn with Nejaunee. I wanted to be sure that she didn't suddenly get worse and I wanted to be with her for the short time we had left. I ached with the sadness of it all. I suppose it was a little foolish to be so distraught over a horse, and yet, there were not many things in this world that I loved more.

I drove to the barn and went in. The warm pleasant smells of horses, sawdust and hay greeted me like an old friend. Nejaunee pricked her ears and looked at me inquisitively. That same look I had seen so many times. I checked all of the horses and topped off the water buckets. I went in to see my new horse, "Buttercup", who was due to foal that April.

I entered the run in shed and sat down in the old cattle trough that ran the length of the wall. Nejaunee walked over to me and searched my pockets for treats. I stood and wrapped my arms around her neck. Thank God she doesn't know, I thought as the tears ran uninhibited now. We stood that way for quite a while. I cried into her neck and explained how I didn't want to do this, but I didn't want her to suffer. I talked about all the good times we had and all of the hardships we had endured. I talked and cried until I felt exhausted. The emotions were taking their toll on me. I sat down again and searched for answers to all of the questions I had. Life and death were so hard to understand.

Throughout the night, I watched my little mare walk in circles looking for a place to lie down. Afraid that she may not be able to get back up, she leaned against a wall. When that didn't work she backed up to the cattle trough and sat in it like a dog might, just to rest her legs. Watching her made me realize that her condition would only get worse. I guess I had been holding out for a glimmer of hope, something that would allow me to change the plans.

It was a long, cold night made even colder by the fear of what I had to face in the morning. Nejaunee would not lie down, so I stood next to her, stroking and soothing her all night.

The morning sun rose brightly and made the snow on the ground glisten. Another time, I would have been thinking of trail rides. That seemed so long ago. A different lifetime.

My father arrived with the trailer and we silently loaded Nejaunee into it. In spite of my father's objections I rode in the trailer with Nejaunee. I needed to be with her. I needed to explain. I needed to relieve this incredible guilt I felt. I felt as though I were betraying her trust in me. We pulled in to the cemetery and unloaded Nejaunee. She nibbled at the grass exposed by the plow along the driveway and seemed in good spirits despite her restless night. I tried not to look at the large hole in the ground a few feet away. The cemetery was filled with beautiful headstones that commemorated the love people felt for their deceased pets. I knew that many others had faced the loss of a dear pet, but it didn't seem to bring me any comfort.

Dr. James pulled in and got out of his truck. He walked to Nejaunee and gently patted her neck. "She's been a good friend to you", he said. That broke whatever control I had and I began to sob.

"You know...She seems better this morning...Maybe we should wait a while", I stammered hoping beyond hope for a reprieve.

"No Lyn, you can't wait. She's going to get worse and waiting will only prolong her suffering. If I thought that there was any chance of improvement I would have told you." Then he told me something that has comforted me ever since.

"We, as humans, wrestle with all of these thoughts and fears of death, but remember, she doesn't know of death. She feels no fear or uncertainty. She knows only what exists at this moment. We are the ones who are left to struggle with our emotions. I promise you she will feel nothing. I will give her a tranquilizer and when she loses consciousness I will give her a drug that will stop her heart. She will die more peacefully than a natural death. A peaceful, pain free death will be your last great gift to her."

I led Nejaunee to the grave and removed her blankets. It was as if I was watching someone else do it. I was numb and felt distant from what was happening. I wrapped my arms around her neck, pressed my face into her mane. "I love you, Nejaunee. You will live in my heart forever. If there is a heaven for me there is a heaven for you and I will see you again. Thank you for everything you have given me. I do this because I love you. I know you would do it for me. Please forgive me. Enthlay sit dou. Abide you here in peace and calmness", I whispered to her.

My father placed his hand on my shoulder and he told me, "we don't have to stay and watch this." I just shook my head. I had to be there with her. Dr. James took a hold of her halter and told me step back. "Sometimes they move a lot during the process, Lyn. It doesn't mean that she feels anything", he said. I stood with my Dad and watched Dr. James insert a needle into her jugular vein. He drew the plunger back and I could see the blood swirl into the syringe. As he depressed the plunger I felt the strength run out of my legs. Nejaunee swayed and as her hind legs gave out, Dr. James pushed on her chest to shift her weight back and she slowly sat down. Then he helped her lower her front end to the ground. I went to her and held her head while he inserted another needle, this one attached to an IV bag. Nejaunee was calm and offered no resistance. As the drug flowed into her she slowly lost consciousness and seemed to go to sleep. I told her over and over what a good girl she was. I wanted that to be her last thought. She gave a great sigh and her breathing stopped. Her lips hung down and her eyes glazed over. Incredible amounts of steam rose from her body, but she made no movement. I buried my face in her neck. I couldn't breathe. I felt briefly as though I might faint. My body jerked with uncontrollable sobs and I cried out in pain. No longer able to maintain any control, I sat in the snow and sobbed with abandon. My father, unable to watch any more, helped me to my feet. I took off her halter and pulled a few hairs from her mane. Dr. James placed his stethoscope to her chest.

"Come on, honey", my father said as he steered me towards the truck.

"No. I want to stay until she's buried", I told him.

"You don't need to watch that", Dr. James said as he stood up, "I know this was hard, but you had to do it. She's at peace now, Lyn."

"How much do I owe you?" my father asked him.

"Please, I could never charge you for this", was his response.

When we arrived home, I went right to my room. My Mother came up after a short while and we sat and cried together. "I wish there was some way I could ease your pain." She said, but we both knew there wasn't anything to be done.

The next few days were very difficult. It was several days before I was capable of returning to work. I carefully hung her halter on my wall and placed her mane hair in a keepsake box on my nightstand. I missed her terribly and visited her grave often. I purchased a headstone for the grave and had it inscribed with the words "Enthlay sit dou", a Native American saying that means, "abide you here in peace and calmness".

A few weeks later, I dreamt of her. She was running through tall grass that waved in the sunlight for as far as the eye could see. The sky was blue and endless. Nejaunee ran past me and kicked out in exuberance. She paused at the top of a hill and turned to me. Her mane and tail moved with the breeze and her eyes shone with youthfulness and spirit. She was fit and happy. She stood looking at me for several moments, and then she shook her head up and down and turned to leave. She looked over her shoulder at me and then slowly trotted over the hill and out of sight. That dream brought me great comfort. I knew that she was well and that she waited for me.

That April, Buttercup delivered a beautiful spotted filly that I own to this day.

Dr. James remained our veterinarian until he retired from his practice. I never received a bill for that day.

My life without Nejaunee will never be the same, but on warm May mornings, when the sun glistens on the dew, I take the day off and go on a trail ride. And I always remember that story about the starfish and the advice *"You can't save them all."* I wonder, that day I walked Nejaunee home, just whose world was saved?

EPILOGUE

It has been twenty-five years since I first met Nejaunee. I still visit her grave and place a wreath there every winter. In all of that time I have had the pleasure of knowing many fine horses. They have taught me many things and have all enriched my life in some way. I met my husband through a common interest in horses and together we built a small training stable that is the center of our lives.

I try to instill in my students the respect and cooperation that I learned from Nejaunee. I can only hope that they achieve the level of satisfaction that I have found working with horses. Nejaunee gave me a gift that I can never fully repay. Nor can I ever repay my parents for believing in me and allowing me to find my way.

Nejaunee taught me compassion for all life by allowing me to see how special her life was to *her* and not just in how it related to my own. She instilled in me a profound belief that animals' lives possess a greater value than what we, as humans, determine them to have. How relieved I was to find, as an adult, so many others who shared my views. Society as a whole is becoming more enlightened. As the' intelligent' animal are we not required by moral law to be the guardians of our fellow creatures?

They're right, I can't save them all, but if by telling our story I give even one person the courage to do what is right, then Nejaunee's memory will live on. Many people do not understand my determination to save that little horse, let alone my love for her. They will never know the bond Nejaunee and I shared. I feel sorry for them; they will never know what I know. There are no words that can express it.

On that January day, many years ago, I lost a being whose very existence helped to define my own.

THE LITTLE BAY MARE

100

LYNDA KAY

ABOUT THE AUTHOR

Lynda Kay was born and raised in a suburb of Buffalo, N.Y. She still resides in upstate New York with her husband and son. They operate a small riding and training stable that is the result of a life-long dream. Their home is filled with a variety of animal companions.

Lynda gratefully acknowledges the tolerance and quiet bemusement of family and friends whenever another wayward animal arrives at her home.

Printed in the United States
1350000001B/427-486

9 781410 760104